TICKS

ROBERT M. HAMILTON

PowerKiDS press.

New York

Published in 2016 by The Rosen Publishing Group, Inc.
29 East 21st Street, New York, NY 10010

First Edition

Editor: Katie Kawa
Book Design: Michael J. Flynn

Photo Credits: Cover, p. 1 (tick) D. Kucharski K. Kucharska/Shutterstock.com; cover, pp. 3–24 (frame) Dinga/Shutterstock.com; p. 4 (scorpion) wacpan/Shutterstock.com; p. 4 (spider) jps/Shutterstock.com; pp. 5, 13 Henrik Larsson/Shutterstock.com; p. 6 veleknez/Shutterstock.com; p. 7 Dr. James L. Castner/Visuals Unlimited/Getty Images; pp. 8, 10, 14, 16, 18, 20 (tick) Melinda Fawver/Shutterstock.com; p. 9 Smileus/Shutterstock.com; p. 11 (all ticks) 3drenderings/Shutterstock.com; p. 12 Jeffrey B. Banke/Shutterstock.com; p. 15 CDC/Science Source/Getty Images; p. 17 Jukka Palm/Shutterstock.com; p. 19 gorillaimages/Shutterstock.com; p. 21 Juergen Faelchle/Shutterstock.com; p. 22 Chris Moody/Shutterstock.com.

Cataloging-in-Publication Data

Hamilton, Robert M.
Ticks / by Robert M. Hamilton.
p. cm. — (Freaky freeloaders: bugs that feed on people)
Includes index.
ISBN 978-1-4994-0767-9 (pbk.)
ISBN 978-1-4994-0769-3 (6 pack)
ISBN 978-1-4994-0770-9 (library binding)
1. Ticks — Juvenile literature. I. Hamilton, Robert M., 1987-. II. Title.
QL458.H36 2016
595.4'29—d23

Manufactured in the United States of America

CPSIA Compliance Information: Batch #WS15PK: For Further Information contact Rosen Publishing, New York, New York at 1-800-237-9932

CONTENTS

WHAT'S A TICK?

If you go on a camping trip, you need to **protect** yourself against ticks. Ticks are parasites. This means they live and feed on the body of another animal, which is called a host. Ticks feed on the blood of their hosts, including people. Ticks can sometimes pass deadly sicknesses to people when they feed on them.

scorpion

Ticks are arachnids, which means they're animals with eight legs and a body formed with two parts. Other arachnids include spiders and scorpions.

spider

FREAKY FACT!
THERE ARE OVER 800 SPECIES, OR KINDS, OF TICKS FOUND AROUND THE WORLD.

Ticks are very small members
of the arachnid family.

THE BLACK-LEGGED TICK

While there are hundreds of species of ticks on Earth, the black-legged tick, which is also known as the deer tick, is perhaps the most feared tick species in the United States. This is because it's the species best known for spreading sicknesses.

Female and male black-legged ticks don't look the same. Adult female black-legged ticks are larger than males. Females are about the size of a sesame seed. Males are dark brown, but females are red with black markings.

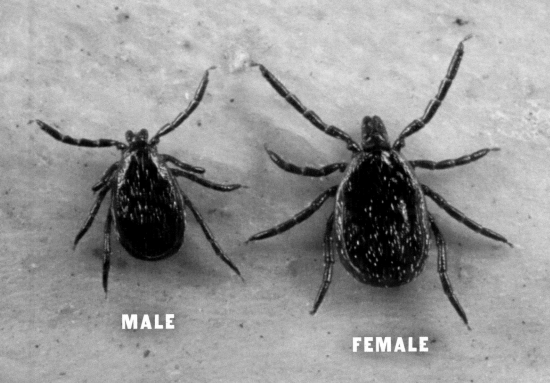

MALE

FEMALE

Black-legged ticks are commonly called deer ticks because deer are a popular host for these parasites.

QUESTING AND BITING

Ticks don't have wings, so they can't fly from one host to another. Instead, they climb onto a host after waiting for one to walk past them. The way ticks wait for a host is called questing.

A tick waits with its lower legs holding onto leaves or tall grass. It reaches out its front legs, so it can quickly crawl onto a passing host. Then, it finds a feeding spot, cuts into the skin, and puts its feeding **tube** into the host.

FREAKY FACT!

SOME TICKS CAN MAKE THEIR HOST FEEL NUMB WHEN THEY BITE THEM. THIS MEANS THE HOST CAN'T FEEL THE TICK ON THEIR SKIN.

It can take anywhere from 10 minutes to two hours for a black-legged tick to get ready to eat once it climbs onto a host.

A TICK'S LIFE CYCLE

A tick's **life cycle** has four basic stages, or steps. A tick starts its life as an egg. Then, a larva comes out of the egg and finds a host. Ticks must feed on blood in order to move from one life cycle stage to the next.

At the end of its time as a larva, a tick molts, or sheds its skin. It then becomes a nymph, which is like a small adult tick. After the nymph feeds and molts again, it becomes an adult.

FREAKY FACT!

ADULT MALE BLACK-LEGGED TICKS DON'T FEED ON BLOOD. HOWEVER, ADULT FEMALES DO. THEY FEED OVER SEVERAL DAYS. THEN, THEY DROP OFF THE HOST, LAY THEIR EGGS, AND DIE.

THE LIFE CYCLE OF A TICK

EGG

- laid by female tick off the body of a host
- often found in piles of fallen leaves

LARVA

- the size of the period at the end of a sentence
- feeds on birds or small **mammals**, such as mice

ADULT

- females are about the size of a sesame seed; males are smaller
- females feed on large mammals; males don't feed on a host
- females die after laying eggs

NYMPH

- about the size of a poppy seed
- looks like dirt or a freckle on a person's skin
- feeds on larger mammals, such as dogs, deer, and people

A tick takes about two years to go from an egg to an adult.

SPREADING DISEASES

Ticks can pick up diseases, or sicknesses, during any stage of their life cycle in which they feed on a host. If a host has **bacteria** living in it that cause certain diseases, the tick can take that bacteria into its body along with the host's blood. Then, it can put the bacteria into its next host.

One disease spread by ticks is Lyme disease. Over 20,000 cases of Lyme disease were reported in the United States in 2013.

TICK AFTER FEEDING

Black-legged ticks spread Lyme disease in the eastern and central parts of the United States. Western black-legged ticks spread the disease in the western part of the country.

LIVING WITH LYME DISEASE

If someone gets Lyme disease from a tick, they can get a **fever**, headache, and other pains within days after being bitten. They can also get a rash—a group of red marks on the skin—that looks like a **bull's-eye**.

If Lyme disease goes untreated, a person could get very painful headaches, pain in their **joints**, changes in their heartbeat, and even brain problems such as short-term memory loss. However, these problems often go away without treatment.

FREAKY FACT!

BLACK-LEGGED TICKS CAN SPREAD OTHER DISEASES TO PEOPLE AS WELL, AND SOME OF THESE DISEASES CAN BE DEADLY. HOWEVER, IF THESE DISEASES ARE DISCOVERED EARLY ENOUGH, THEY ALL CAN BE TREATED.

Lyme disease can be treated with drugs, but people often don't need treatment for it. In some cases, though, people still have health problems even after being treated for Lyme disease.

DANGEROUS DOG TICKS

Another kind of tick known for spreading diseases in the United States is the American dog tick. This tick is found throughout the country in areas east of the Rocky Mountains, but it's also found in smaller numbers in the western United States.

The American dog tick can spread a disease called Rocky Mountain spotted fever. This disease causes fever, headaches, body pains, and other health problems. It needs to be treated quickly, because it can be deadly.

The American dog tick is larger than the
black-legged tick.

BE SAFE IN THE WOODS

How can you keep yourself safe from ticks and the diseases they could be carrying? Be careful when walking in wooded areas with tall grasses, especially in the late spring and summer, which is when ticks are most active. If you're going to be in areas where ticks live, use special bug sprays and wear pants and long-sleeved shirts.

If you think a tick could have crawled on you, take a bath or shower as soon as you can. Then, check your body for ticks.

If your pet was in an area where ticks might live, check them for these parasites, too. Ticks can crawl onto people from the body of their pet. Ticks can also move from a person's clothing to their body, so put clothing in the dryer to kill ticks.

GET IT OFF!

If you do find a tick on your body, it's important to remove it as soon as possible. In most cases of Lyme disease, the tick must be on a person's skin for 24 to 48 hours before the bacteria that causes the sickness enters the body.

A person should use tweezers to take a tick off someone's body. They should pull upward with a steady motion. If they twist the tick, the tick's feeding tube could stay stuck in the skin.

FREAKY FACT!

DON'T CRUSH A TICK WITH YOUR FINGERS. A TICK COULD STILL SPREAD DISEASE THROUGH A CUT—EVEN ONE THAT'S TOO SMALL FOR YOU TO SEE.

Tweezers are an important tool to have in your home in case you become a host for a tick.

TRICKY TICKS

Don't let their tiny size fool you—ticks can be big pests. They can feed on your blood, and sometimes they can make you sick.

Lyme disease is one of the fastest-growing diseases spread by parasites in the United States. However, this disease can be treated by a doctor, and sometimes the signs of the disease can go away on their own. Ticks may seem scary, but knowing more about these parasites helps us be better prepared to deal with them.

GLOSSARY

bacteria: Living things made up of one cell, many of which cause sickness.

bull's-eye: The center of a target in sports such as archery, shooting, and darts.

fever: A rise above a person's usual body temperature.

joint: The point in an animal's body where two bones come together.

life cycle: The steps that a living thing goes through as it grows and dies.

mammal: Any warm-blooded animal whose babies drink milk and whose body is covered with hair or fur.

protect: To keep safe.

tube: A long, hollow object that can carry a liquid.

INDEX

A
adult, 6, 10, 11
American dog tick, 16, 17
arachnids, 4, 5

B
bacteria, 12, 20
black-legged tick, 6, 7, 9, 10, 13, 14, 17

D
deer tick, 6, 7
diseases, 12, 14, 16, 18, 20, 22

E
egg, 10, 11

F
feeding tube, 8, 20

H
host, 4, 7, 8, 9, 10, 11, 12, 21

L
larva, 10, 11
life cycle, 10, 11, 12
Lyme disease, 12, 13, 14, 15, 20, 22

M
mammals, 11

N
nymph, 10, 11

Q
questing, 8

R
Rocky Mountain spotted fever, 16

T
tweezers, 20, 21

W
western black-legged ticks, 13

WEBSITES

Due to the changing nature of Internet links, PowerKids Press has developed an online list of websites related to the subject of this book. This site is updated regularly. Please use this link to access the list: www.powerkidslinks.com/bfp/tick